CW00689291

SKY HIGH

NORFOLK COAST

AN AERIAL JOURNEY

MIKE PAGE

HALSGROVE

First published in Great Britain in 2008

British Library Cataloguing-in-Publication Data
A CIP record for this title is available from the British Library

ISBN 978 1 84114 830 4

HALSGROVE
Halsgrove House
Ryelands Industrial Estate
Bagley Road, Wellington
Somerset TA21 9PZ
Tel: 01823 653777
Fax: 01823 216796
email: sales@halsgrove.com
website: www.halsgrove.com

Printed and bound by Grafiche Flaminia, Italy

Introduction

The unique nature of the Norfolk coastline, its visual beauty set against its susceptibility to change through manmade and environmental effects, holds a particular fascination when seen from the air. The photographs in this book provide views which cover all aspects of the coast, from its sweeping isolation, to tiny seaside villages, and to the popular and populated resorts of Cromer and Great Yarmouth.

In this book the reader is offered a visual memento of the Norfolk coast through photographs specially selected by the author. Both for those who know this part of Norfolk well, or for those who are visiting on holiday, this gem of a book provides the perfect keepsake.

Mike Page's books include: *A Broads Eye View; A Broads Eye View 2; The Norfolk Coast from the Air; The Suffolk Coast from the Air; Spirit of the Norfolk Broads.*

The River Yare flows along Breydon Water and through Great Yarmouth before joining the North Sea at the harbour mouth.   Gorleston is in the foreground.

The South Denes (to the right of picture) once housed a racecourse and a First World War Royal Naval Air Service base. Now the area is dominated by Great Yarmouth's Power Station which is fired by North Sea Gas.

Work has started on a new Outer Harbour.

Opposite:
For many years the Haven lifting Bridge was the
only river crossing in Great Yarmouth. The splendid
square red brick Victorian building is the Town Hall.

Scroby Windfarm.
Wind turbines appearing
through a sea mist

These Powergen turbines
stand 60 metres high, their
foundations are piled up to
30 metres into the sea bed.

The 30 wind turbines are on Scroby Sands. Over the centuries
many ships have run aground on these sandbanks.

The fishing village of Caister has provided and manned a lifeboat for nearly 200 years.

Norfolk's own California, so called because a hoard of gold coins thought to have been washed up from a sunken ship was discovered at the base of the cliffs around the time of the Californian Gold Rush (1849).

Hemsby beach with the Somerton wind turbines beyond.

Opposite:
Hemsby village. Caravan sites and Holiday Villages
abound all along the Norfolk coast.

Horsey Mere is only a mile from the coast and if the
sea broke through here as it did in 1953 then much of
Broadland would be flooded with salt water.

Opposite:
Marram grass has been planted on the dunes behind
Winterton beach to combat wind and wave erosion.

Grey seals at Horsey. Massive boulders have been
imported to reduce the scouring action of the waves.

Opposite:
Horsey Mill (NT) used to drain the marshes but an electric
pump in the shed at the side does the job now.

Happisburgh is one of the villages most at risk from inundation by the sea.
Cliff falls happen every winter.

Left:
Happisburgh 1997.

Above: Happisburgh 2007.

Storm surge damage at Walcott.

Opposite:
When the sea gets too rough the
Police close the road here at Walcott.

Concrete defences are holding the sea back at Bacton.

Opposite:
The coming of the railway turned Mundesley into a popular
seaside village. On the horizon is the 'golf ball' at RAF
Trimingham, it was part of the early warning radar system.

The Coastwatch building has a good vantage point at the top of the slope.
There's a great deal of shipping passing along this coast.

Cliff falls at Trimingham.

Several wealthy people built large holiday homes here
at Overstrand at the turn of the last century.

There's a cliff top walk from Overstrand to Cromer.

The tallest church tower in Norfolk (160 feet).

Opposite:
Cromer lighthouse has been here since 1833
although there were earlier ones on the site. Before that
a light in the church tower served as a landmark.

At the end of the pier work is on going to house a new lifeboat.

Caravans abound at
East Runton...

...and West Runton

31

Sheringham, once a fishing village now a resort.

Opposite:
Beeston Bump, the Norfolk Coast Long Distance
Footpath runs right across the top.

Sheringham Golf Course is getting smaller as the cliffs erode.

Opposite:
There's a good natured rivalry between Cromer and Sheringham. Sheringham locals are referred to as 'Shannocks' by the Cromer locals, 'shanny' or 'shaddock' means 'rowdy'.

Sheringham at the coast and the village of Upper Sheringham,
with its church in the foreground.

The North Norfolk Railway runs between Sheringham and Holt and passes through lovely countryside…and yet another golf course.

Railway sidings and workshops of the
North Norfolk Railway at Weybourne.

Opposite:
Weybourne village and mill, in the distance is the home of the
Muckleburgh Collection of army tanks and military memorabilia.

Salthouse. Until five centuries ago the sea came up
to the higher ground. Boats set out from here to
sail as far as Iceland to catch cod and herring.

Opposite:
Storm surge damage November 2007.

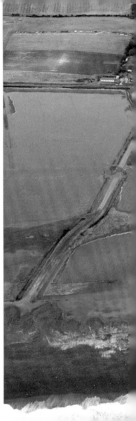

Cley village and marshes. The mill is now a Guest House but until
the end of the First World War it ground corn.

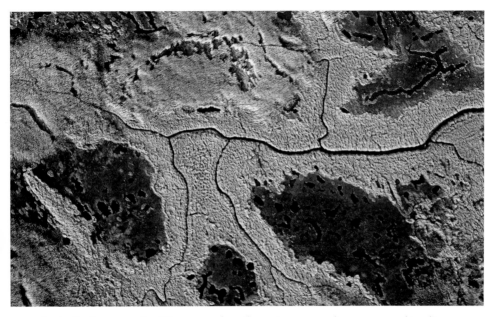

Fantastic shapes on the Glaven marshes, the watercourses show up as snaking lines.

Since the marshes were drained, Blakeney like Salthouse is
a village further from the sea than it used to be.

Opposite:
The villages of Cley and Blakeney with the vista stretching
to Blakeney Point and the saltmarshes beyond.

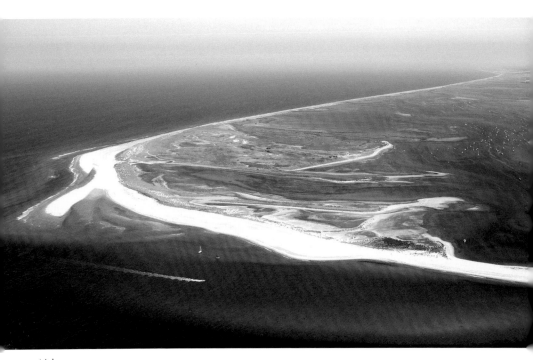

Seals on the point appear to take no notice of the boating activity.

Opposite:
High tide at Blakeney Point. The Point is a shingle spit
which over the last thousand years has doubled in length
because its materials gradually are being moved westwards
by the action of wind and tide.

Blakeney Point at high tide.

Morston and Stiffkey. Samphire, an edible plant but
an acquired taste, grows here in abundance.

Wells next the Sea, once an important port.

The entrance to Wells harbour. This is the only harbour for sea-going ships between Great Yarmouth and Kings Lynn.

Wells Harbour. The Harbourmaster's Office is in the foreground. The former granary (centre) recently has been converted to flats.

Holkham Hall. The lake is the remnant of a saltwater creek.

Burnham Overy. Staithe – 'staithe' is an old English
word meaning a landing place.

Scolt Head is said to be so called because the sand hills are said to resemble ringworm on a skull (scolt).

Brancaster Staithe – a mecca for small sailing boats.

Brancaster is a mile away from Brancaster Staithe (seen in the background). At Brancaster the Romans had a fort called Branodunum where troops assembled for the voyage home.

Titchwell's RSPB Reserve provides a winter roost for Hen Harriers and Marsh Harriers.
The marshes were farmed until the 1953 floods destroyed the sea wall.

Thornham village with the marshes beyond was once a port handling coal in and grain out
until the railways destroyed the trade. There's no land between here and the North Pole.

Holme Dunes Reserve (Norfolk Wildlife Trust) is one of the nearest landfalls for migratory birds flying south from the Arctic Circle and Greenland.

Fantastic shapes in Holme's saltmarshes can best be seen from the air.

Old Hunstanton (foreground) is quite separate from New Hunstanton (the latter generally referred to simply as Hunstanton or Hunston). It was created as a holiday resort in the mid nineteenth century. On a clear day the Lincolnshire coast can be seen across The Wash.

The lighthouse functioned until 1921. It's now a private residence.

Paragliders get the necessary lift from the cliffs of the Norfolk Coast.

The distinctive striped Hunstanton cliffs are fossil rich glacial deposits of white chalk, red ironstone and yellow carrstone.